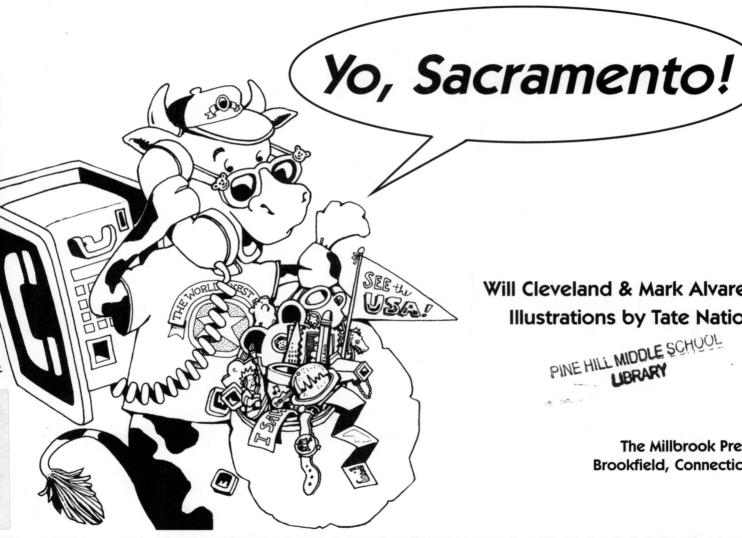

Yo, Sacramento!

Will Cleveland & Mark Alvarez
Illustrations by Tate Nation

The Millbrook Press
Brookfield, Connecticut

Cover illustration: Tate Nation
Cover design: Paul F. Rossmann
Book design: Deborah Fillion
Copyright © 1994, 1997 by Goodwood Press
Published in 1997 by The Millbrook Press
2 Old New Milford Road, Brookfield, Connecticut 06804

Printed in the United States of America
5 4 3 2 1

Library of Congress Cataloging-in-Publication Data
Cleveland, Will.
Yo, Sacramento! : and all those other state capitals you don't know / Will Cleveland and
Mark Alvarez.
p.   cm .
Summary: Presents facts about each state with cartoon-style illustrations to serve as
memory aids for the state capitals and quizzes to reinforce information.
ISBN 0-7613-0252-2 (lib. bdg.). — ISBN 0-7613-0237-9 (pbk.)
1. United States—Geography—Juvenile literature. 2. Capitals
(Cities)—United States—Juvenile literature. [1. United States—Geography—
Miscellanea. 2. Capitals (Cities)] I. Alvarez, Mark. II. Title.
E161.3.C44 1997
973—dc20   96-42099   CIP   AC

★

For Jeanne and Audrey

with lots of love and laughs.

T.N.

Introduction

My wife, Anne, will not let our three children listen to a Walkman when we go on family trips in the car. She insists that we have "quality time." During such a trip not too long ago, I sat driving, enveloped by the heavy silence, regretting that we were not making more "constructive" use of our time. All of sudden, like a bolt of pure inspiration, it struck me that we should ... memorize the Presidents!

I got a list from the encyclopedia and, over the next few trips, my children, Braden, Meg, and Will, made up the memory techniques that allow anyone to memorize all the Presidents in twenty minutes. Later, one of Meg's friends was traveling with us and I insisted on "teaching" her all the Presidents. She was so excited at how easy it all was that she recited them the next day to her class. After that, whenever one of my children's friends would come by the house, I would take them into the living room and teach them to recite the Presi-dents in twenty minutes. It worked so well that two things happened: First, it led to the creation of our first book, *Yo, Millard Fillmore!* And second, my children's friends stopped coming by the house.

Since *Yo, Millard Fillmore!* came out, Tate Nation, Mark Alvarez, and I have hit the lecture circuit speaking to Library Associations, Reading Councils, and schools about the memory techniques used in the book. Our presentations have been received enthusiastically by educators and students, who keep asking for a similar book to help learn the states and their capitals. So here's *Yo, Sacramento!*

Mark writes all of the history on the Presidents and the states. Tate spends thousands of hours preparing the illustrations and my kids thought up the memory tricks. Yet, I get to have my name listed first on the book. Is this a great country, or what?

— *Will Cleveland*

★ ★ Contents ★ ★

How to Use This Book

Just look at the cartoons and read the little stories next to them. Then take the short test at the end of each section. That's all there is to it. Each picture has two parts. One of the parts looks like the way the capital sounds and the other looks like the way the state sounds. That way, when you say the state's name, you will be reminded of the picture that sounds like the state. When you remember that picture, you will also remember the part of the picture that sounds like the capital's name.

...boys eat a hoe.
(Boise, Idaho)

For instance, the capital of New Hampshire
is Concord. The cartoon shows a nude
hamster, which sounds like
New Hampshire, riding
on the Concorde jet.
When you think of New
Hampshire, you'll see in your
mind the picture of the nude hamster and
remember that he's riding the Concorde.

Once you know all the states and their
capitals, you can go back and read about
each of them on the left page. We think you'll
find them pretty interesting.

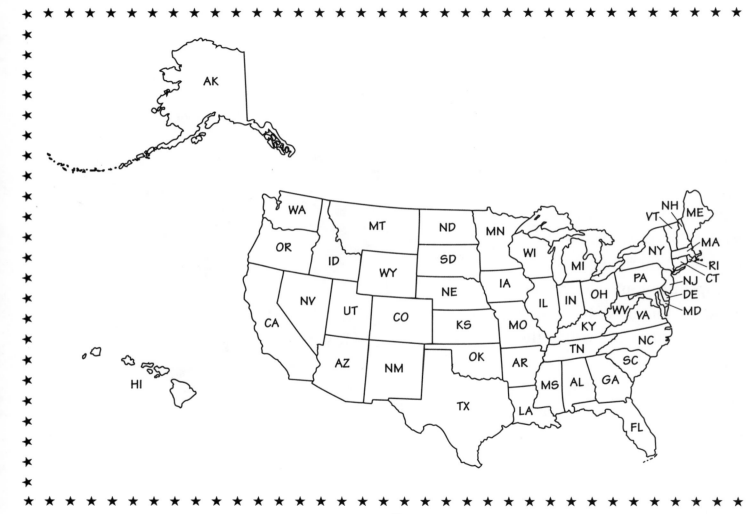

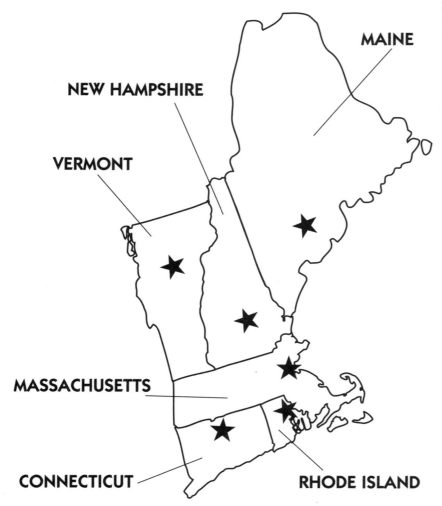

MAINE

NEW HAMPSHIRE

VERMONT

MASSACHUSETTS

CONNECTICUT

RHODE ISLAND

New England

Tucked up in the far northeast corner of the U.S., New England landscapes run the gamut from seashore to deep woods to fierce and rugged mountains. There are lots of cities here, but there are many small towns, too, and most of them still have Town Meetings, where citizens vote on the major issues facing them. It is a form of pure democracy that exists in few other parts of the country—or the world.

Connecticut
(CT)

Capital: Hartford
State Bird: Robin
State Flower: Mountain Laurel
State Tree: White Oak

5th state to enter the Union (January 9, 1788) ★ 48th largest state

One of the most famous Americans of the mid-1800s was P.T. Barnum. He was born in Bethel, and lived much of his life in Bridgeport.

Barnum is usually called a "showman," because he built a vast fortune by promoting and displaying things—things people might not have known they wanted to see until Barnum persuaded them they did. For over 20 years, he ran the American Museum in New York, where many of his displays were, simply, fakes. Barnum even called himself, "Prince of the Humbugs."

When crowds got heavy at the museum, and Barnum wanted to move people through quickly, he hung up a sign that said, To The Egress. People who followed the directions expecting to see a weird animal or strange exhibit found themselves back on the street—"Egress" means "exit."

Barnum got rich when he became the manager of a midget named Charles S. Stratton, whom he called General Tom Thumb. He took the General on a European tour, met with all manner or royalty, and raked in the loot. Barnum later managed the American tour of Jenny Lind, "the Swedish nightingale," who was probably the most popular singer of the century. He eventually started a circus that he called "The Greatest Show on Earth," the slogan its successor, the Ringling Brothers and Barnum & Bailey Circus, still uses.

Hartford, Connecticut

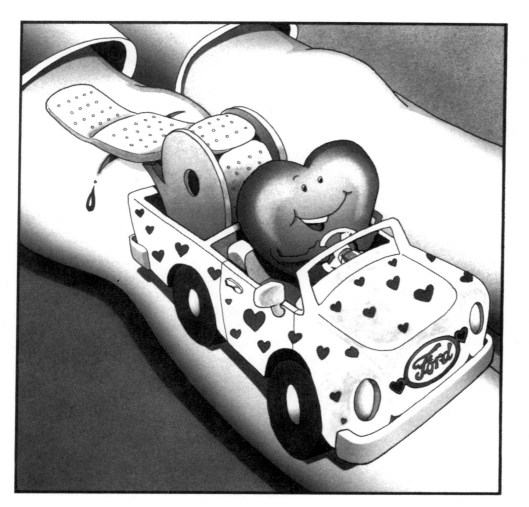

Don't cry if you get scratched. The **heart** in the **Ford** will drive by and **connect a cut**.

The **heart Ford** (Hartford) will **connect a cut** (Connecticut).

Maine
(ME)

Capital: Augusta
State Bird: Chickadee
State Flower: White Pine Cone and Tassel
State Tree: White Pine

23rd state to enter the Union (March 15, 1820) ★ 39th largest state

In July of 1863, the Confederate Army of Northern Virginia ran into the Federal Army of the Potomac at a little town in Pennsylvania named Gettysburg. This accidental meeting sparked a three-day battle that is often called the turning point of the Civil War. On the second day of the battle, southern troops planned to attack the far left end of the northern army, defeat it, and then "roll up" the whole northern line.

At that far left end of the line were stationed the men of the Twentieth Maine Regiment, commanded by Colonel Joshua Lawrence Chamberlain, who had been a college professor when the war began. They fought off many southern attacks, until they ran out of ammunition. Then Chamberlain gave the command to fix bayonets, and led his remaining men in a charge. The southern soldiers, who had lost hundreds of men in their attacks, and who were tired and worn out, ran away or surrendered. The left wing of the northern army had held, and the south had no chance to defeat the Federal Army that day. The next morning, northern troops hurled back Pickett's Charge, and won the battle.

Maine is proud to this day that its men may have saved the Union. After the war, Chamberlain was elected governor of the state. He is one of the greatest heroes of a war that produced many on both sides.

Head is the eastern-most point in the U.S. ★ When you travel north up the rugged coast of Maine, you're said to be going

4

Augusta, Maine

Hold onto your hat, **a** mighty **gust of** wind is blowing down **Main** Street!

A gust of (Augusta) wind on **Main** (Maine) Street.

Massachusetts

(MA)

Capital: Boston
State Bird: Chickadee
State Flower: Mayflower
State Tree: American Elm

6th state to enter the Union (February 6, 1788) ★ 45th largest state

---

You know the poem about Paul Revere's ride, don't you? "'Twas the eighteenth of April in seventy-five…One if by land, two if by sea…" and all that? It's a terrific poem that tells of Revere's warning to the colonists that the British Redcoats were on the march. But Revere wasn't the only man who carried the message that "The British are coming!" that night. William Dawes and Samuel Prescott had also been sent into the countryside.

Robert Newman, sexton of Christ Church (what we now call North Church) did hang two lanterns in the belfry, but the signal was received by Colonel Conant in Charlestown before Revere actually made it across the Charles River.

On a small, quick horse he later called "very good," Revere rode toward Lexington, spreading the alarm. Once there, he met Dawes and Prescott, and the three of them headed for Concord. Revere never made it. He was detained by a British patrol and his mount was taken from him. He walked back to Lexington and was dragging a trunk of vital papers belonging to John Hancock across the Green to safety when the British arrived to confront the local Minute Men and the "shot heard 'round the world" was fired to start the American Revolution.

You can still see and visit Paul Revere's house in Boston's north end.

Boston, Massachusetts

A city made of boxes is called Box Town. In the center of **Box Town** is a **massive chess set**.

Box Town (Boston) surrounds a **massive chess set** (Massachusetts).

New Hampshire
(NH)

Capital: Concord
State Bird: Purple Finch
State Flower: Purple Lilac
State Tree: White Birch

9th state to enter the Union (June 21, 1788) ★ 44th largest state

Mount Washington, in New Hampshire's White Mountains, is the highest peak in the northeast. It's part of the Presidential Range, in which you'll find summits named after both Adamses, Jefferson, Madison, Monroe, Jackson, and many others, right up to Eisenhower.

This is rugged country, well above the tree-line, but at 6,288 feet, Mount Washington doesn't seem to measure up to the 14,000-footers of the West, let alone the 20,000 feet of Denali in Alaska. And it even has a road and a cog railway to its top, where, on pleasant summer days, you'll find many cars, lots of people, and plenty of souvenirs to buy.

But Mount Washington is not to be trifled with. Its weather is famous, changeable, and vicious. Even in summer, temperatures can plummet toward freezing, mists can roll in, and hikers can be put to the severest tests. And in the winter—watch out! The weather is often unendurable by humans. The highest wind speed ever recorded on earth blew here: 231 miles per hour—and then the wind gauge blew away!

Concord, New Hampshire

Fasten your seat belt, a **nude hamster** is riding atop the **Concorde**!

The **Concorde** (Concord) is being flown by a **nude hamster** (New Hampshire).

Rhode Island

(RI)

Capital: Providence
State Bird: Rhode Island Red
State Flower: Violet
State Tree: Red Maple

13th state to enter the Union (May 29, 1790) ★ 50th largest state

The Puritans came to Massachusetts for religious freedom. But for them, that didn't include religious freedom for others. They persecuted those who didn't believe as they did. In doing so, they caused the founding of Rhode Island.

Roger Williams came to Massachusetts with his family in 1630, and was a preacher in several towns. But he had strange ideas. He thought, for one thing, that people should be able to worship as they please. For another, he thought it was wrong to steal land from the Indians. For these and other "dangerous opinions," Williams was banished from the Massachusetts Bay Colony. He went south, where he was temporarily taken in and cared for by an Indian band led by Massasoit, who had years before welcomed the Pilgrims to Plymouth. Eventually, Williams bought land from the Narragansetts and established a village that would become Providence. Soon after, Anne Hutchinson was forced to flee from Massachusetts for her religious beliefs. She was welcomed by Williams, who helped her buy land and establish the town that became Portsmouth.

People in other colonies called Rhode Island "a chaos of all religions," and "Rogue Island," but these two pioneers of religious freedom set a tone of tolerance in Rhode Island that was eventually written into our Bill of Rights.

Providence, Rhode Island

On the **road island**, all the prophets are having a dance—a **prophet dance**.

A **prophet dance** (Providence) on a **road island** (Rhode Island).

Vermont
(VT)

Capital: Montpelier
State Bird: Hermit Thrush
State Flower: Red Clover
State Tree: Sugar Maple

14th state to enter the Union (March 4, 1791) ★ 43rd largest state

Ethan Allen was born in Connecticut, but he became the most famous and colorful figure in Vermont history. Vermont wasn't an original colony, but was known as "the New Hampshire Grants," because the government of New Hampshire granted land there to settlers. In 1764, the British decided that the area belonged to New York, and that New Hampshire land grants were invalid. Allen and other settlers weren't about to pay for their land twice, so they resisted. The famous Green Mountain Boys were essentially a gang of grantsmen who terrorized "Yorkers" and fought off attempts to enforce the new arrangement. Ethan Allen, the loudest and pushiest among them, was their leader. New York leaders offered a reward of 20 pounds for his arrest.

When the Revolution came, Allen and the Boys, along with Benedict Arnold (years before he became a traitor) captured Fort Ticonderoga from a small and surprised British garrison. Allen was later captured in the attack on Quebec, and wrote a famous account of his cruel imprisonment. After his release in 1778, Allen still couldn't get the Continental Congress to recognize Vermont as a state…so he turned around and began to negotiate with the British. He was accused of treason, but the charges were never pressed. Allen died two years before Vermont became the fourteenth State.

Montpelier, Vermont

Watch out when you go mountain climbing, a gigantic **varmint** is peeling away layers of the mountain with his **mountain peeler**.

A **mountain peeler** (Montpelier) **varmint** (Vermont).

Let's try this little review.

What can the heart Ford do for you?

On what street is the gust of wind blowing?

What's in the center of Box Town?

What's riding on the Concorde?

Where are they having the prophet dance?

 Who has a mountain peeler?

Who can drive out and connect a cut?

 What's the weather like on Main Street?

In what city will you find the massive chess set?

What type of jet does the nude hamster ride on?

 What type of dance is held on the road island?

What's the varmint doing?

PENNSYLVANIA

NEW YORK

NEW JERSEY

DELAWARE

MARYLAND

Middle Atlantic

Three of the Middle Atlantic states—New York, New Jersey, and Pennsylvania—are among our most populous, and are definitely "northern" in character. Delaware and Maryland, on the other hand, are less heavily populated and are border states, with a more southern feel. Generally speaking, this is an industrial part of the country, but any region that encompasses the Allegheny Mountains, New York City, and Chesapeake Bay is clearly very diverse. This is true of most of the regions in the U.S.

Delaware
(DE)

Capital: Dover
State Bird: Blue Hen Chicken
State Flower: Peach Blossom
State Tree: American Holly

1st state to enter the Union (December 7, 1787) ★ 49th largest state

We've all heard of Paul Revere's Ride, but the most famous event in Delaware history is Caesar Rodney's Ride.

Rodney was a delegate from the Delaware counties to the Continental Congress of 1776. He returned home to help put down a threat by Tories who were gathering to fight for the king. Back in Philadelphia, the two remaining Delaware delegates were split on the issue of whether or not to support the Declaration of Independence. Rodney was needed to break the tie.

Legend has it that Tories intercepted a series of messages sent to Rodney by his colleagues in Congress, but that, at the last possible minute, he got the news from a black maid who smuggled it in to him. Although many thought he couldn't possibly make it to Philadelphia on time, he jumped on his horse (or into his carriage—historians are still arguing about this) and galloped off. He stopped only to change exhausted horses on his way, and made the 90-mile trip in the nick of time. He voted for independence.

Eleven years later, Delaware became "the First State" by ratifying the Constitution before any of the other former colonies.

Dover, Delaware

Sometimes delicatessen owners just can't seem to get along and they have a deli war. Maybe the **dove over** the **deli war** will bring peace.

A **dove over** (Dover) the **deli war** (Delaware).

Annapolis ★ Sharpsburg in 1862 remains the bloodiest day in American military history

by Catholics ★ Named in honor of Queen Henrietta Maria, of England ★ Francis Scott

Maryland

(MD)

Capital: Annapolis
State Bird: Baltimore Oriole
State Flower: Black-Eyed Susan
State Tree: White Oak

7th state to enter the Union (April 28, 1788) ★ 42nd largest state

In September of 1814, the British were attacking up the Chesapeake Bay, and one of their objectives was the city of Baltimore. They had captured an American named William Beanes, and two of his friends wanted to get him released. John Skinner and Francis Scott Key arrived in Baltimore Harbor and won their friend's freedom, but the British told them they'd have to stay on board a prisoner-exchange ship until after the attack.

The Americans had asked Mrs. Mary Pickersgill to make a huge American flag—over 50 feet long—to fly above the fort. A great British bombardment began on September 13, and lasted all day and all night. It included, not just cannon balls and shells, but Congreave rockets, which trailed through the sky and left a red glare in their wake. Through the smoke and haze and darkness, Key and his friends couldn't see what was happening. As the mist cleared early in the morning of the 14th, they could see a flag waving above Fort McHenry, and they soon realized it wasn't the British ensign, but Mrs. Pickersgill's star-spangled banner.

Key was so moved he sat down on the spot and wrote the poem that was eventually set to music and became our national anthem. The huge flag still exists, and you can see it at the Museum of History and Technology in Washington, D.C.

Key's grandson was arrested and imprisoned in Fort McHenry during the Civil War ★ The battle at Antietam Creek near

Annapolis, Maryland

All the girls are named Mary so they call the place **Mary land**. They're all taking a nap and you'd better not wake them or you'll get in trouble with the **nap police**.

A nap police (Annapolis) in **Mary land** (Maryland).

New Jersey

(NJ)

Capital: Trenton
State Bird: Eastern Goldfinch
State Flower: Purple Violet
State Tree: Red Oak

3rd state to enter the Union (December 18, 1787) ★ 46th largest state

---

When the Revolutionary War began, a man named William Franklin was the governor of New Jersey. He was a London-trained lawyer, and as events led toward war, he supported the British, so he was what was known as a Loyalist (because he was loyal to the king), or a Tory.

He was also the son of Benjamin Franklin.

Needless to say, father and son, who had been very close most of William's life, did not see eye to eye on political matters. In 1776, William was arrested by Revolutionary officials, and he was sent to a horrible, vermin-ridden jail in Connecticut, far beyond the reach of those who might try to

rescue him. His father, Benjamin Franklin, didn't try to help him. In fact, his father made sure he was closely watched, and that he was not exchanged for prisoners held by the British.

When William was finally freed in 1778, he went to New York, where the British Army had its headquarters. There he began to take his revenge by seeing to the execution of a number of prisoners held by the British.

After the war, William Franklin spent the rest of his life in England, and never reconciled with his father. Benjamin Franklin, great American statesman, seldom mentioned his son again.

20

Trenton, New Jersey

The engineer on **train ten** gives out **new jerseys** to the football team.

Train ten (Trenton) brings **new jerseys** (New Jersey).

New York
(NY)

Capital: Albany
State Bird: Bluebird
State Flower: Rose
State Tree: Sugar Maple

11th state to enter the Union (July 26, 1788) ★ 30th largest state

The U.S. has always been a country of immigrants, but the tide from Europe was especially strong in the last half of the last century and the first few years of this one. Between 1892 and 1924, most people coming to the United States sailed into New York Harbor, glided past the Statue of Liberty, docked in Manhattan, were off-loaded into barges, and were ferried to Ellis Island.

Here, they walked under a large canopy into a huge building, picked up their belongings in the Baggage Hall, and then moved into the Great Hall, where doctors and inspectors processed up to 10,000 people a day. Immigrants had to be healthy,

so everyone was examined. Most people—about 80 percent—passed, but those who didn't were deported—sent back to the country they'd come from. This rejection often caused terrible anguish. Imagine how families felt when one member could not be allowed in.

About a third of the people who passed through Ellis Island stayed in the New York area. The rest, of many nationalities and religions, fanned out across the country, looking, as new Americans always had, for a place to put down roots, live a decent life, and savor the freedom of the new world.

Albany,
New York

The **owl** and **bunny** sure like riding on the brand **new yak**.

An **owl** and **bunny** (Albany) on a **new yak** (New York).

23

Pennsylvania
(PA)

Capital: Harrisburg
State Bird: Ruffed Grouse
State Flower: Mountain Laurel
State Tree: Hemlock

2nd state to enter the Union (December 12, 1787) ★ 33rd largest state

During the Revolution, armies didn't campaign against each other during the winter—it was too hard to get around. The winter of 1777–1778 was an especially difficult one for the Americans. The British had taken Philadelphia, forcing Congress to flee, and General Washington had established his winter camp at Valley Forge.

During a fierce winter, the Americans faced their first, but by no means their last, great test of misery. Thousands of soldiers died of cold, hunger, and disease. Farmers in the countryside seemed much more eager to sell food for gold to the British in Philadelphia than for Continental dollars to the starving army at Valley forge.

Washington feared a mutiny. Instead, he got a better-drilled army. Baron von Steuben (who wasn't really a Baron, but who was a highly professional soldier) arrived in February to teach military skills to the poorly-trained Americans. Morale improved, though conditions didn't. Washington broke camp in June. He and his army faced many more dark days before defeating Cornwallis at Yorktown, but Valley Forge became the symbol of hardships overcome.

Harrisburg, Pennsylvania

Which way is the wind blowing? Well, look up at the **hairy bird** on the **pencil vane**.

A **hairy bird** (Harrisburg) on the **pencil vane** (Pennsylvania).

Let's see what you remember.

 What is the peace dove over, that he might have a chance of stopping?

Where do the nap police patrol?

 What does train ten give out to the team?

What do the owl and bunny ride on?

What type of vane does the hairy bird sit on?

What flies over the deli war?

 Who will arrest you for making noise in Mary land?

Which train brings the new jerseys?

 What two animals ride on the new yak?

What type of bird sits on the pencil vane?

WEST VIRGINIA

VIRGINIA

KENTUCKY

TENNESSEE

NORTH
CAROLINA

ARKANSAS

SOUTH
CAROLINA

GEORGIA

FLORIDA

ALABAMA

LOUISIANA

MISSISSIPPI

South

With a few exceptions, this region is made up of "the old Confederacy." The exceptions are Kentucky and West Virginia, which are included but never seceded from the Union, and Texas, which seceded from the Union but isn't included. Parts of the South have been industrialized for years, but much of the region remained agricultural and relatively poor while other parts of the country boomed. This is changing quickly.

Alabama
(AL)

Capital: Montgomery
State Bird: Yellowhammer
State Flower: Camellia
State Tree: Southern Pine

22nd state to enter the Union (December 14, 1819) ★ 29th largest state

In July 1941, twelve men began training at Tuskegee to become Army Air Force combat fliers. That doesn't sound like a big deal does it? We were soon to enter World War II, and millions of men would be training to be fliers, sailors, Marines, and soldiers.

But these men were black, and they were the first African Americans ever taught to be fighter pilots. Many white people at that time didn't think black men had the courage or the will to perform under danger and pressure. The Tuskeegee airmen proved them wrong, as their fathers and grandfathers had done during the Revolution, the Civil War, and as "Buffalo Soldiers" on the frontier.

The first segregated outfits were deployed to North Africa in April of 1943. From that point to the end of the war, they compiled an outstanding record, flying 1,600 combat missions, 15,000 sorties, and shooting down almost 600 enemy planes.

One of the main jobs of the Tuskegee airmen was to protect American bombers during their missions over Italy and other parts of Europe. During the whole war, the Tuskeegee airmen never lost a single bomber to an enemy plane. Benjamin O. Davis, their commander, became the first African-American general. President Harry S Truman ordered the integration of the Armed Forces in 1948.

Montgomery, Alabama

Ali Baba found a treasure in the magic **mountain of gum**.

A **mountain of gum** (Montgomery) holds **Ali Baba**'s (Alabama) treasure.

Arkansas
(AR)

Capital: Little Rock
State Bird: Mockingbird
State Flower: Apple Blossom
State Tree: Pine

25th state to enter the Union (June 15, 1836) ★ 27th largest state

In 1906, a man named John M. Huddleston picked up a few stones from his farm three miles outside Murfreesboro, and took them to a jeweler in town. Huddleston knew he had something out of the ordinary, but both men were astonished to find that the stones were diamonds.

Once the word got out, the area vibrated with excitement. Within two years, investors had bought Huddleston's farm for $38,000—a small fortune in 1908—and got about the business of mining. For the next 17 years they extracted gems from the only diamond mine in the United States. A few of the stones were very fine, high-quality gems suitable for jewelry, although most were good only for industrial purposes. (Diamonds are among the hardest substances known to man, and are often used to cut or abrade metals.) After 1925, the mine was no longer making its investors enough money, and it was closed.

Nowadays, the site is called Crater of Diamonds State Park. It is open to the public, and if you pay a fee, you can hunt for diamonds yourself.

Little Rock, Arkansas

Did you know that an **ark can saw** a **little rock**?

A **little rock** (Little Rock) that an **ark can saw** (Arkansas).

Florida
(FL)

Capital: Tallahassee
State Bird: Mockingbird
State Flower: Orange Blossom
State Tree: Sabal Palm

27th state to enter the Union (March 3, 1845) ★ 22nd largest state

The Indians most associated with Florida are the Seminoles, who actually were Creeks who moved south late in the 1700s. The Seminoles welcomed fleeing slaves, and Andrew Jackson attacked them in the First Seminole War in 1817 in an attempt to recapture these runaways.

The Seminoles were driven south, and were given a reservation near Lake Okeechobee. By the 1830s, white settlers wanted that land, and the Second Seminole War began. It was expensive for both sides. The U.S. lost 2,000 soldiers and spent about $50 million. For the Seminoles it was even worse. They lost their land when their leader,

Osceola, was captured when he agreed to a meeting under a flag of truce. The tribe was forced onto the "trail of tears" to "Indian Territory" in Oklahoma. The trail got its name from the Cherokees who called it *Nunna dual Tsunyi*, "the trail where we cried," because thousands of their people died of disease and hunger as they were marched west by the U.S. military.

A Third Seminole War broke out in the 1850s, when the government wanted to clear out the few remaining bands of Indians. The most "troublesome" were paid by the U.S. to join their relatives who had already made the trek to Oklahoma.

Tallahassee, Florida

The **taller Lassie** stands on a **floor of dots** while the shorter Lassie is on a plain floor.

A **taller Lassie** (Tallahassee) is on a **floor of dots** (Florida).

Georgia
(GA)

Capital: Atlanta
State Bird: Brown Thrasher
State Flower: Cherokee Rose
State Tree: Live Oak

4th state to enter the Union (January 2, 1788) ★ 21st largest state

Eli Whitney got rich as the inventor of mass production, in which relatively unskilled workers assemble products out of parts that are all exactly alike. But he is most famous as the inventor of the cotton gin. In the early 1790s, he was staying on the plantation of Catherine Greene, widow of Nathaniel Greene, a famous Revolutionary War general. He learned that planters could sell all the cotton they had to textile mills in England. There was a problem, though. It took forever to separate the desirable cotton fibers from the unwanted cotton seeds.

Whitney quickly designed a simple machine in which wires plucked the fibers from the seed pod. This didn't quite do the trick, though. The fibers still had to be stripped by hand from the wires. Catherine Greene suggested adding a brush to the apparatus. With this modification, the cotton gin was complete. Cotton soon became King in the South and—tragically—planters turned more and more to slave labor to raise and harvest their crops.

Catherine Greene's contribution in perfecting the cotton gin is forgotten by almost everyone. Maybe this is because she was a woman. Maybe it's because Whitney's reputation grew so large in later years. Whatever the reason, there's no reason for *us* not to remember her.

· JUDGE HAT · LANTERN ·

Atlanta, Georgia

How would you like to be tried in court where there is a **hat lantern** doing the **judging**?

The **hat lantern** (Atlanta) is in court **judging** (Georgia).

Kentucky
(KY)

Capital: Frankfort
State Bird: Kentucky Cardinal
State Flower: Goldenrod
State Tree: Kentucky Coffeetree

15th state to enter the Union (June 1, 1792) ★ 37th largest state

Have you ever stopped to think what's under your feet? In parts of Kentucky, you can't help but wonder. The bedrock in large areas of the state is limestone, which is relatively soft, and which reacts chemically to dissolve in mildly acidic water.

This process, going on for millions of years, has formed Mammoth Cave, which is part of Mammoth Cave National Park. The cave was discovered in 1799 by a hunter who was tracking a wounded animal. Combined with the Flint Ridge cave system, to which it's connected, the Mammoth Cave system is the longest we know of.

Because Mammoth Cave has a constant temperature of 54 degrees, it "inhales" when the outside temperature is higher and "exhales" when the outside temperature is lower.

At Mammoth Cave, you can see underground rivers, lakes, and waterfalls, as well as colorful, oddly shaped rock formations. As a visitor, you can see about 12 miles of Mammoth Cave, and you can descend as far as 360 feet below ground level. But that's just a small part of the whole system, in which over 200 miles of passages have been explored. People who explore caves are called "spelunkers."

Frankfort, Kentucky

To keep it from being eaten too soon, the **frank fort** protects the **canned turkey**.

A **frank fort** (Frankfort) protects a **canned turkey** (Kentucky).

Louisiana
(LA)

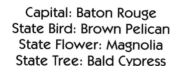

Capital: Baton Rouge
State Bird: Brown Pelican
State Flower: Magnolia
State Tree: Bald Cypress

18th state to enter the Union (April 30, 1812) ★ 31st largest state

The only state ★ Acadians who were expelled from their homes in Canada by the British

means "red stick," and the story is that French explorers found a red stick driven into the

During the war of 1812, the British wanted access to the Mississippi River. To get it, they had to take New Orleans, where General Andrew Jackson had been assigned to hold them off. Jackson had about 1,000 regular troops, 2,000 militiamen of varying quality, and the services of smuggler Jean Lafitte and his crews. There were actually several battles around New Orleans from late December, 1814, through early January, 1815, as the British General Pakenham tried to defeat the force his superiors called "the contemptible Dirty Shirts."

In the final British assault, Pakenham had over 6,000 troops to use. He sent his main force directly against the barricades Jackson's men had built of cotton bales, planks, and mud. These troops were veterans of the brutal campaigns of the Napoleonic Wars in Europe. They were brave, well-trained, and used to success against the best army in the world. But over 2,000 of them were killed in a series of assaults. Pakenham himself was shot out of the saddle, mortally wounded. The Americans, well protected behind their barricades, lost only seven men. It was one of the worst defeats ever suffered by the British Army. And it was all for nothing—the peace treaty had been signed two weeks before, but word hadn't made it across the ocean yet.

The Cajuns, whose cooking has become so popular, are the descendants of the ★ ground there to mark Indian tribal boundaries

Baton Rouge, Louisiana

The roach never could hit! Once again, the **batting roach loses an inning**.

The **batting roach** (Baton Rouge) **loses an inning** (Louisiana).

Mississippi

(MS)

Capital: Jackson
State Bird: Mockingbird
State Flower: Magnolia
State Tree: Magnolia

20th state to enter the Union (December 10, 1817) ★ 32nd largest state

Mississippi's most famous statesman was also for a few years the most hated man in the United States. Jefferson Davis was the President of the Confederacy during the Civil War. He was born in Kentucky, but was brought to Mississippi as a baby. He grew up at Rosemount Plantation in Wilkinson County, and eventually established his own plantation, Briarfield. Davis was a soldier and politician who eventually became a Congressman, a Senator, and Secretary of War, before becoming a Senator again. He was the strongest and most respected spokesman of the South during the debates over states rights and the extension of slavery into the territories.

When Mississippi seceded, Davis resigned from the Senate and went home, hoping to be named to head the new Confederate army. Instead, he was named President. He was a dignified man of absolute integrity, but he was a rigid man, and he had many bitter opponents even in the South.

As the war ended, Davis fled south, hoping to reach Cuba, from which he could start a new life. He was captured by the Union Army, which falsely accused him of disguising himself as a woman, and imprisoned for two years, under indictment for treason. He was eventually freed, and lived out most of his last years at "Beauvoir," which you can visit near Biloxi.

De Soto and La Salle both explored through the Mississippi region ★ 47-day siege before surrendering the city to General Grant in 1863 ★

in 1962 ★ Choctaw, Chickasaw, and Natchez Indians were the area's original inhabitants

Jackson, Mississippi

No matter how much the little guy tries, the **jack's son** always **misses a sip of tea**.

The **jack's son** (Jackson) **misses a sip of tea** (Mississippi).

North Carolina

(NC)

Capital: Raleigh
State Bird: Cardinal
State Flower: Flowering Dogwood
State Tree: Pine

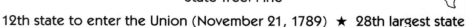

12th state to enter the Union (November 21, 1789) ★ 28th largest state

---

Okay, you know that the Wright brothers made their first flight at Kitty Hawk but do you know why? This area, on North Carolina's Outer Banks, has wide beaches, high, soft hills of sand, and—most important of all—constant winds.

Airplanes fly because their wings are shaped to create "lift" as air passes over them. For their low-powered, slow-moving machine, the Wrights needed a steady, strong, and reliable breeze to fly their plane into if they hoped to create enough lift to get off the ground. They sailed gliders at Kitty Hawk for several years, experimenting with wing forms and learning lessons they would incorporate into their first airplane.

Wilbur and Orville Wright ran a bicycle shop in Dayton, Ohio. They had never graduated from high school, but they read everything they could about flight.

On the morning of December 17, 1903, Orville climbed onto the wing of their 745-pound biplane. As the 12-horsepower engine moved the wheel-less plane off its rail and into the air, Wilbur ran alongside to keep the 40-foot wing steady. The first flight lasted only 12 seconds and spanned about 120 feet—less than half the length of a football field. The brothers took turns flying through the day, and by the end of the afternoon they had stretched their longest flight to 59 seconds and 852 feet.

Raleigh, North Carolina

Norse carrots line up in front of the crowd at a pep **rally**.

At the **rally** (Raleigh) the **Norse carrots line up** (North Carolina).

South Carolina
(SC)

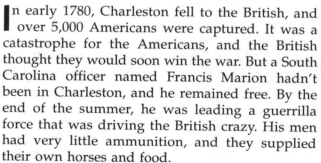

Capital: Columbia
State Bird: Carolina Wren
State Flower: Carolina Jessamine
State Tree: Palmetto

8th state to enter the Union (May 23, 1788) ★ 40th largest state

In early 1780, Charleston fell to the British, and over 5,000 Americans were captured. It was a catastrophe for the Americans, and the British thought they would soon win the war. But a South Carolina officer named Francis Marion hadn't been in Charleston, and he remained free. By the end of the summer, he was leading a guerrilla force that was driving the British crazy. His men had very little ammunition, and they supplied their own horses and food.

Marion knew the countryside, and he combined his formal training as a soldier with his understanding of "Indian-style" fighting to become one of the great guerrilla fighters in American history.

Marion and his men would hit the British sharply, often at night, and always at a vulnerable point, then escape back to the rivers, swamps, bogs, and tangles they knew so well. Marion's main refuge was on Snow Island in the Pee Dee River. The British commander finally ordered the famous British cavalry colonel Banastre Tarleton to follow Marion, find him, and capture him. Tarleton did his best, but finally gave up after tracking through the terrible terrain. It was he who gave the South Carolinian his nickname: "The Swamp Fox."

Columbia, South Carolina

When it gets real cold sows don't like walking through a cold lumber yard and they don't like being crowded. So, **sow carriers line up** in a **cold lumber yard**.

In a **cold lumber yard** (Columbia) **sow carriers line up** (South Carolina).

45

Tennessee
(TN)

Capital: Nashville
State Bird: Mockingbird
State Flower: Iris
State Tree: Tulip Poplar

16th state to enter the Union (June 1, 1796) ★ 34th largest state

"**B**orn on a mountaintop in Tennessee...." Actually, as much as we love Davy Crockett, Tennessee's most famous legend, there's much better music than this available in the Volunteer State.

Tennessee is full of music. Elvis Presley, of course, was raised in Memphis, and built the fabulous Graceland there. But Memphis had its own music long before Elvis came along. It's often called "the home of the blues," which makes it one of the homes of jazz, rock, and folk music, too. W.C. Handy's most famous piece may be the *St. Louis Blues*, but he wrote the *Memphis Blues* first. Beale Street, now renewed, is still worth a trip.

Halfway across the state, Nashville is the home of country music. The Grand Ole Opry started there in 1925, and was broadcast weekly for years from Ryman Auditorium downtown. The show moved to Opryland—a big, glossy entertainment park—in 1974, and continues as country music's premier showcase. A restored Ryman reopened in 1994, and is once again home to good singin' and pickin'. These are all great places to visit.

Nashville, Tennessee

The sharks like to **gnash** the **veal** served at the **tent at sea**.

Sharks **gnash veal** (Nashville) by the **tent at sea** (Tennessee).

Virginia
(VA)

Capital: Richmond
State Bird: Cardinal
State Flower: Dogwood
State Tree: Dogwood

10th state to enter the Union (June 25, 1788) ★ 36th largest state

During the American Revolution, there had been bitter fighting all through the South during 1780 and 1781. Lord Cornwallis, who commanded British troops in that region, eventually decided to move north. In August of 1781, Cornwallis led his army into Virginia, to Yorktown. He expected to be resupplied by ships coming from the British headquarters in New York. But the French fleet, led by Admiral De Grasse, beat off the British ships. At about the same time, the joint American and French army led by George Washington surrounded Yorktown and laid siege to Cornwallis' army. After two weeks of battering, Cornwallis surrendered his 8,000 troops. As they marched out to stack their weapons, British musicians played a tune called "The World Turned Upside Down." You can still see the trenches the armies dug at Yorktown over 200 years ago.

It's interesting to think about two things. First, Washington couldn't have won at Yorktown without the aid of the French. And second, the defeat at Yorktown didn't destroy the British militarily. It simply forced a change in the political landscape in London, because the Prime Minister resigned. The new cabinet decided to negotiate with the Americans, and a final treaty was signed in 1783.

★ In 1619, the first slaves in British North America were brought to Virginia ★ In 1607, Jamestown at made was World New

48

Richmond, Virginia

A **fur genie** grants the wishes of a **rich man**.

A **rich man**
(Richmond) and his
fur genie (Virginia).

49

West Virginia
(WV)

Capital: Charleston
State Bird: Cardinal
State Flower: Rhododendron
State Tree: Sugar Maple

35th state to enter the Union (June 20, 1863) ★ 41st largest state

---

In 1859, a man who gave his name as Isaac Smith rented property across the Potomac River from Harpers Ferry, in what is now West Virginia. This man was, in fact, John Brown, a famous—some would say infamous—opponent of slavery in the United States. Brown and his family had been involved in the bitter violence over slavery in the Kansas Territory, and he was now watching Harpers Ferry because he had an idea for an event that would trigger slave revolt throughout the southern states.

On October 16, Brown and 18 others, including several of his sons, attacked and occupied the federal arsenal at Harpers Ferry. They expected slaves to rise and flock to them to be armed. They were mistaken. Locals pinned down the raiding party in the building and called for help. A company of Marines under army colonel Robert E. Lee arrived and stormed the little band in the arsenal. John Brown was wounded, captured, and tried for treason. He was hanged on December 2, and immediately became a martyr to the cause of abolition. His actions and his death focused attention, not just on the institution of slavery, but on what sort of blood and struggle it might take to eradicate it.

Many historians date the true beginning of the Civil War to Brown's raid on Harpers Ferry.

Charleston, West Virginia

We don't know why he cooks them so long and then throws them away, but the **wasteful genie** likes to **char stones**.

Charred stones (Charleston) cooked by a **wasteful genie** (West Virginia).

Let's review the southern states.

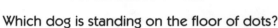

Who hides his treasure in the mountain of gum?

Where does Ali Baba hide his treasure?

Who can do what to a little rock?

An ark can saw what?

 Where does the taller Lassie stand?

Which dog is standing on the floor of dots?

What does the hat lantern do in court?

What kind of lantern does the judging in court?

What does the frank fort protect
so it won't get eaten too early?

What's protecting the canned turkey?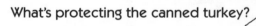

What is the batting roach doing when he strikes out?

Who's always losing an inning?

What does the jack's son do
when he tries to drink politely?

Who misses a sip of tea
no matter how hard he tries not to?

At the rally, who lines up in front of the crowd?

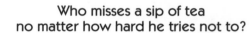 At what do the Norse carrots line up
for people to cheer?

Who will you see in a line up in a cold lumber yard?

Where do the sow carriers line up?

 Where do the sharks get to gnash veal?

What do the sharks do to what's served
on the tent at sea?

Who grants the wishes of a rich man?

For whom does the genie grant wishes?

Who cooks and then throws away
the charred stones?

What does the wasteful genie like to cook
and then throw away?

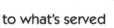

NORTH DAKOTA

MINNESOTA

SOUTH
DAKOTA

WISCONSIN

MICHIGAN

NEBRASKA

IOWA

KANSAS

ILLINOIS

MISSOURI

INDIANA

OHIO

Midwest

Generally speaking, this is a great agricultural area, with states like Iowa, Kansas, Nebraska, and parts of others making up the nation's "breadbasket." But there's lots of industry and many big cities in the upper midwest around the Great Lakes, as well as rugged woods and lakes in the far north.

Illinois
(IL)

Capital: Springfield
State Bird: Cardinal
State Flower: Native Violet
State Tree: White Oak

21st state to enter the Union (December 3, 1818) ★ 24th largest state

In 1893, Chicago held the World's Columbian Exhibition. Most of the buildings for this world's fair were white and columned—built to look as if they might have come from ancient Greece or Rome. So the Transportation Building, long, low and arched, with a colorful entry that came to be called the "Golden Door," stood out.

Its designer was Louis Sullivan, one of America's great architects, and one of the important members of what has come to be called "the Chicago School." Sullivan's idea was that the form of a building—what it looked like—should be dictated by its *function*—what it was supposed to do. He detested the idea that a bank building, for example, should look like a temple to Zeus. He and his partner Dankmar Adler, had already designed a number of buildings that are now considered masterpieces of American architecture. Some, like the Auditorium, can still be seen in Chicago.

Today, Louis Sullivan is remembered most often for being an early employer of another great architect, Frank Lloyd Wright. But many of his projects have become American classics, and he deserves to stand alone, near the very top of his profession.

Springfield, Illinois

If you don't like complaining, cover your ears. In the **spring field** all you'll hear is **ill noises**.

In the **spring field** (Springfield) you'll hear **ill noises** (Illinois).

Indiana
(IN)

Capital: Indianapolis
State Bird: Cardinal
State Flower: Peony
State Tree: Tulip Tree

19th state to enter the Union (December 11, 1816) ★ 38th largest state

You know the slogan "Tippecanoe and Tyler, too," don't you? It had a lot to do with the victory of William Henry Harrison in the 1840 Presidential election. But, you may ask, what is all this Tippecanoe business?

Way back in 1811, Harrison had been the governor of what was then Indiana Territory (which included much more than the current state of Indiana). Tecumseh was trying to rally the Indians of the area to get together and fight the encroaching whites. Harrison moved to put a stop to the Indian threat. In the first week of November, he camped on the Tippecanoe River, near the camp of Tecum-

seh's brother, who was called the Prophet. The next day, the Indians attacked. In a brutal fight, both sides suffered serious losses (Harrison's troops actually lost more men than the Indians), but the Prophet and his men were driven off. Harrison reported that he had inflicted the worst defeat on the Indians "since their acquaintance with the white people." This wasn't true, but it made Harrison's reputation anyway.

Once he was elected President, Harrison gave a long inaugural speech in bad weather, caught pneumonia, and was dead in a month. He was our shortest-serving President.

Indianapolis, Indiana

They don't have to fight anymore. The **Indian ant** is sharing the peace pipe with the **Indian apples**.

Indian apples (Indianapolis) take the peace pipe from the **Indian ant** (Indiana).

Called ★ the topsoil is over 600 feet deep ★ In some parts of Iowa, the people are farmers

Iowa
(IA)

Capital: Des Moines
State Bird: Eastern Goldfinch
State Flower: Wild Rose
State Tree: Oak

29th state to enter the Union (December 28, 1846) ★ 25th largest state

western boundary is the Missouri ★ Most of the state was prairie in pioneer days ★ Birthplace of President Herbert Hoover

Young William Sunday of Nevada, Iowa, was a fine baseball player. He was so good that he was eventually signed to play for the great Chicago White Stockings of the National League—a club run by another Iowan, Adrian "Cap" Anson of Marshalltown, who is now a member of the Baseball Hall of Fame.

Sunday was a very speedy runner, and he was an immediate success as an outfielder and baserunner, although he never developed into much of a hitter.

Ballplayers in those days were a rough and ready lot. Most were poorly educated, and many were alcoholics. Sunday was different, though,

and gradually earned the nickname "Parson" among his teammates and around the league. After the 1890 season, he quit baseball and took a job at the YMCA. Before long, he had hit the road, preaching the gospel in tents and halls.

He became famous for the physical nature of his preaching. He'd wave his arms, jump around the stage, and—always a crowd favorite—run full-tilt across the stage and throw himself into the kind of slide he used when he was stealing bases for Chicago. He used his baseball career as a source of lessons and stories, and Billy Sunday quickly became—and remained for many years— the best known evangelist in the land.

Des Moines, Iowa

After spending all **day mowing** a path to the library, it's closed when he finally gets there. "Oh no, my book is overdue," he thinks. "Now, **I owe a** fine!"

After all **day mowing** (Des Moines) he thinks, "**I owe a** (Iowa) fine."

Kansas

(KS)

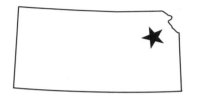

Capital: Topeka
State Bird: Western Meadow Lark
State Flower: Sunflower
State Tree: Cottonwood

34th state to enter the Union (January 29, 1861) ★ 14th largest state

During the 1890s, a big, strong woman from Kansas named Carry Nation became the most famous woman in the United States. An actress? Nope. A writer? Nope. A politician? Not too many women in that line back then. Carry Nation made herself famous—infamous, really—by smashing up saloons.

In her younger days, she had been married to an alcoholic, and after she moved to Kansas with her new husband, she found that the state's prohibition laws were not being enforced. She decided to enforce them herself, and began a campaign of destruction that made her and her axe familiar images to Americans.

Carry Nation took her campaign outside of Kansas, and was arrested a number of times for breaking up saloons in states where drinking was legal. She was the best known member of what was called the temperance movement (few of whose members were as violent as she was), which ultimately succeeded in passing an amendment to the Constitution which made drinking alcohol illegal throughout the United States. This amendment was very unpopular in many parts of the country. During the "Roaring '20s" lots of people broke the law to drink anyway, and the amendment was repealed after only 14 years in 1933.

Topeka, Kansas

He's so shy, look at the **toe peeking** around the **cans of S**'s.

A **toe peeking** (Topeka) around **cans of S**'s (Kansas).

Michigan
(MI)

Capital: Lansing
State Bird: Robin
State Flower: Apple Blossom
State Tree: White Pine

26th state to enter the Union (January 26, 1837) ★ 23rd largest state

Michigan is the center of the American car industry. Its most important early figure was Henry Ford, who established the Ford Motor Company in 1903.

Although his company had terrible labor troubles in the 1930s, Ford began as an enlightened employer. In 1914, when the going wage was under $2 for a 9-hour day, he offered his adult workers $5 for an 8-hour day. He wanted his workers to feel secure, and to have enough money to buy the product they were making.

That product, in those days, was the famous Model T, a simple, cheap, well-made car that began selling for $850 in 1908, but that cost only $360 in 1916. Ford could lower his prices on the "Tin Lizzie" because he had developed the first moving assembly line, which allowed quick, efficient mass production.

Ford was a good friend of Thomas Edison, who had encouraged him to work on his "horseless carriage" back in the 1890s. The two became vacation neighbors, and Ford gave Edison a 1917 Model T that was upgraded over the next ten years every time the designers or engineers back in Detroit made an advance. The result is a unique automobile that was Edison's favorite, and that can still be seen at the Edison/Ford Winter Estates in Fort Myers, Florida.

Lansing, Michigan

One of the **lambs singing** to the wolves is nervous because he's **missing a gun**.

A **lamb singing** (Lansing) is **missing a gun** (Michigan).

Minnesota
(MN)

Capital: St. Paul
State Bird: Common Loon
State Flower: Pink and White Lady's Slipper
State Tree: Norway Pine

32nd state to enter the Union (May 11, 1858) ★ 12th largest state

In 1898, a farmer from Kensington named Olof Ohman claimed to have dug up a stone on his farm that was covered with ancient writings, called *runes*. The "Kensington Rune Stone" was studied by experts, who made this translation:

"Eight Goths [Swedes] and twenty-two Norwegians, on a journey of discovery from Vinland westward. We camp by two skarries [islands] one day's journey north of this stone. We were out fishing one day. When we returned home, we found ten men red of blood and dead. Ave Virgo Maria. Save us from evil" There were more runes on the edge of the stone: "[We] have ten men by the sea to look after our ships fourteen days' journeys from this island. [In the] year [of our Lord] 1362."

Many people believed that this was proof of Viking explorations in North America long before Columbus. But the Kensington Rune Stone, now kept by the Chamber of Commerce of Alexandria, is today believed to be a hoax, perpetrated by Ohman, a local schoolmaster named Sven Fogelblad, and a neighbor, John Gran. They all hoped to have a good laugh at the highly educated scholars they could fool into believing in the stone. They certainly got what they were after.

St. Paul, Minnesota

Saint Paul did not need to worry about getting thirsty because along the road there were **many sodas**.

Saint Paul (St. Paul) walked by **many sodas** (Minnesota).

Missouri
(MO)

Capital: Jefferson City
State Bird: Bluebird
State Flower: Hawthorn
State Tree: Flowering Dogwood

24th state to enter the Union (August 10, 1821) ★ 19th largest state

You know Tom Sawyer and Huckleberry Finn, right? They are the two best-known characters created by Mark Twain, whose real name was Samuel Langhorne Clemens.

Sam Clemens grew up in Hannibal, Missouri, and he used this childhood setting as the model for St. Petersburg, the hometown of his two young heroes. Just as they did, he and his friends spent a lot of time on the river, watching it carry odd and interesting things downstream during flood season. There were real-life models of Huckleberry Finn and Becky Thatcher.

When Sam Clemens grew up, he headed to South America to make his fortune, but on the way down river, he decided he wanted to be a riverboat pilot instead. He persuaded the pilot of the boat he was on to teach him the ropes, and for several years he held the job that every boy along the Mississippi River dreamed of.

Sam Clemens later traveled all over the world, and he lived in many places, but his life would have been much different if he hadn't begun as a young Missouri boy on the river bank.

Jefferson City, Missouri

His dad punished him for making a mess and now the **chef's son** is **sitting** in **misery** after ruining the meal.

Chef's son sitting (Jefferson City) in **misery** (Missouri).

67

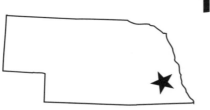

Nebraska
(NE)

Capital: Lincoln
State Bird: Western Meadow Lark
State Flower: Goldenrod
State Tree: Cottonwood

37th state to enter the Union (March 1, 1867) ★ **15th largest state**

Willa Cather grew up in Red Cloud during the 1880s. Her family moved there from Virginia when she was nine years old. There were no schools near her family's ranch, so she studied at home. When she was a teenager, her family moved to town where she attended Red Cloud High School. After graduating from the University of Nebraska in 1895, she worked as a journalist and a teacher before becoming an author of short stories and novels.

Cather is best known for her books about Nebraska frontier life. *O Pioneers!* and *My Antonia* are her best known works, and they used to be read by most high school students in the U.S. They are sadly neglected today, but almost any youngster looking for a good read and interesting characters would enjoy them. Cather won the Pulitzer Prize for a book called *One of Ours* in 1921.

As much as she loved the spirit of the pioneers, Cather also wrote about how hard it can be for someone with ambition and talent to break out of the drudgery and hard work of country and small-town life to pursue her dreams. That's a feeling many of us have from time to time, and it is another reason why many young readers enjoy the books of Willa Cather.

the candidates don't run on the Republican or Democratic tickets ★ The Platte River was a pathway to the west ★ The largest

68

Lincoln, Nebraska

Happy birthday, Abe! Abraham **Lincoln** gets a **new brass key**.

Lincoln (Lincoln) gets a **new brass key** (Nebraska).

North Dakota

(ND)

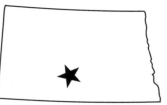

Capital: **Bismarck**
State Bird: **Western Meadow Lark**
State Flower: **Wild Prairie Rose**
State Tree: **American Elm**

39th state to enter the Union (November 2, 1889) ★ **17th largest state**

You know Teddy Roosevelt, right? Rough Rider? President? Face on Mount Rushmore?

Over a decade before he became the youngest President, Theodore Roosevelt was a cattle rancher in what would become North Dakota. He had worked hard to strengthen himself during and after a sickly childhood, but it was out west that he won the battle and became the husky, rugged, and powerful man we see in pictures of the Rough Rider or the President.

As a rancher, TR spent days at a time in the saddle, in all weather, participating in round-ups, hunting, and scouting the country. He also became a real wild west character.

Once, in Nolan's Hotel in Mingusville, he knocked out a bully who had pulled his pistols, called him "four eyes," and tried to make him go for drinks. Another time, Roosevelt and a small posse chased three men who had stolen a boat and set off down the Little Missouri River. They captured the thieves, and Roosevelt—staying awake for 36 straight hours so he could keep his eyes on the bad guys—brought them 150 miles back to jail in Mandan.

This rough and tough experience is what gave Roosevelt the idea for the Rough Riders, and when he formed the regiment for the Spanish-American War, it was full of cowboys.

Bismarck,
North Dakota

You're allowed only just so many **Norse Ducks** for your **quota**, so make sure the counter **bees mark** the numbers correctly.

Bees mark (Bismarck) the numbers for the **Norse Duck quota** (North Dakota).

Ohio
(OH)

Capital: Columbus
State Bird: Cardinal
State Flower: Scarlet Carnation
State Tree: Buckeye

17th state to enter the Union (March 1, 1803) ★ 35th largest state

In 1869, a Cincinnati businessman named Champion decided to give his city the best baseball team in the land. To do this, he broke the rules of the day and openly paid his players. The result was a team—the Cincinnati Red Stockings—that toured the country from East Coast to West, played the best clubs in every city, and didn't lose a game all year. It was the sport's first great team, and it began the era of professional baseball that eventually led to the National and American Leagues. Cincinnati is, rightly, considered the birthplace of professional baseball.

Football also has a home in Ohio. About a half-century later, a group of midwesterners decided it was time to organize professional football. The league they began soon evolved into the National Football League. Many of the early professional teams sprang from Ohio's smaller cities. The Canton Bulldogs is perhaps the best remembered of these fabled clubs, and Canton today is the home of the Pro Football Hall Of Fame.

Ohio has a lot going for it. Seven Presidents—Grant, Hayes, Garfield, Benjamin Harrison, McKinley, Taft, and Harding—were born here. So were the Wright Brothers. But it's fascinating that two of our three main American professional sports also call the state home.

Columbus, Ohio

Columbus, the explorer, was so startled at what he saw, that he said, "**Oh**" to the **high O**.

Columbus (Columbus) said, "**Oh, high O**" (Ohio).

South Dakota

(SD)

Capital: Pierre
State Bird: Ring-necked Pheasant
State Flower: American Pasqueflower
State Tree: Black Hills Spruce

40th state to enter the Union (November 2, 1889) ★ 16th largest state

When "Wild Bill" Hickock arrived to mine gold in the boomtown of Deadwood City in 1876, he had already become famous as the man who cleaned up Hayes City and Abiline, Kansas. He was a tough guy with a quick trigger finger, and he was in the right place. Deadwood was full of gamblers, grifters, and scoundrels of all kinds, hoping to make a killing off of the men working the new gold fields.

Hickock was playing poker in the Bella Union Saloon one day, sitting with his back to the door, which friends said he'd never done before. A drunken small-time crook called Broken-Nose Jack McCall thought he could make his name by killing the famous gunfighter. He walked into the saloon, came up behind Wild Bill, pulled a gun, and shot him dead. Supposedly, Hickock was holding aces and eights in his card hand, and to this day, that's known as "the dead man's hand."

You can see James Butler Hickock's grave in the Mount Moriah Cemetery today. It's said that Calamity Jane helped bury him.

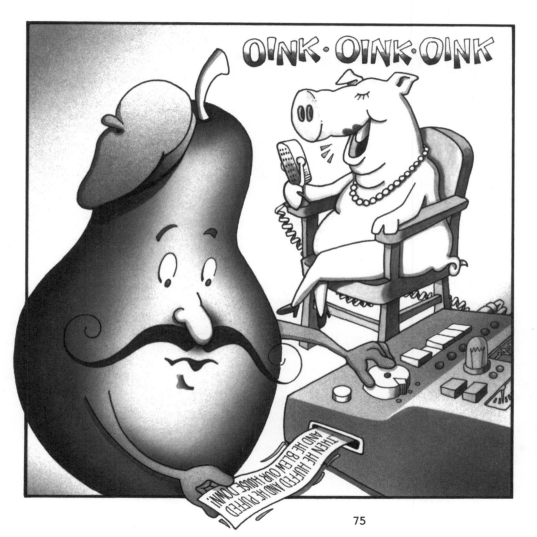

Pierre, South Dakota

The **pear** is a French inspector named **Pierre** and wants to understand what the sow says, so he uses a **sow decoder**.

Pierre the **pear** (Pierre) uses a **sow decoder** (South Dakota).

Wisconsin
(WI)

Capital: Madison
State Bird: Robin
State Flower: Wood Violet
State Tree: Sugar Maple

30th state to enter the Union (May 29, 1848) ★ 26th largest state

You know that song about Mrs. O'Leary's cow kicking over the lantern and starting the Great Chicago Fire? Well, on the very same day—October 8, 1871—Wisconsin experienced the Peshtigo Forest Fire. The woods had been drying out all summer, and the people of Wisconsin and all of the woodland midwest were worried about fire. When it finally happened, it was spectacular and deadly. Eight-hundred people in the small town of Peshtigo were killed when the town seemed to explode into a firestorm. Those who survived made for the nearby river, and spent hours there, up to their necks, watching their town burn to the ground. One of them said, "I saw nothing but flames; houses, trees, and the air itself were on fire."

More than four times as many people were killed in the Wisconsin fire than died in Chicago, but Peshtigo was a lot farther away from trains, telegraphs, and newspapers, though, so it took a lot longer for people to hear about the forest fire, and few people remember it today.

Madison, Wisconsin

The **medicine whips** the **con's son** if he misbehaves like his dad.

Medicine (Madison) **whips** the **con's son** (Wisconsin).

Let's go over the midwestern states.

What sounds are made in the spring field?

Where do you hear nothing but ill noises?

Who do the Indian apples take the peace pipe from?

Who does the Indian ant give the peace pipe to?

 What does the boy think when he's late after spending all day mowing to the library?

How has the boy spent his day when he gets to the library and thinks, "I owe a fine."

What type of cans is the toe peeking around?

Who is doing what around the cans of S's?

Why is the lamb singing nervously?

Who is missing a gun?

What will Saint Paul find along the road to quench his thirst?

Who walks down the road with many sodas?

Who is in misery when he messes up the stove? Is he standing or sitting?

What sad mood is the chef's son sitting in?

Who gets a new brass key on his birthday?

What does Lincoln get for his birthday?

Who does what to keep track of the Norse duck quota?

For what type of quota do the bees mark?

What does Columbus say at the letter in the air?

Who says "Oh, high O" from the deck of his ship?

What does Pierre the pear use to understand the animal he's questioning?

Who operates the sow decoder as part of his investigation?

What does the medicine do for punishment and to whom?

What type of bottle whips the con's son when he's been bad?

78

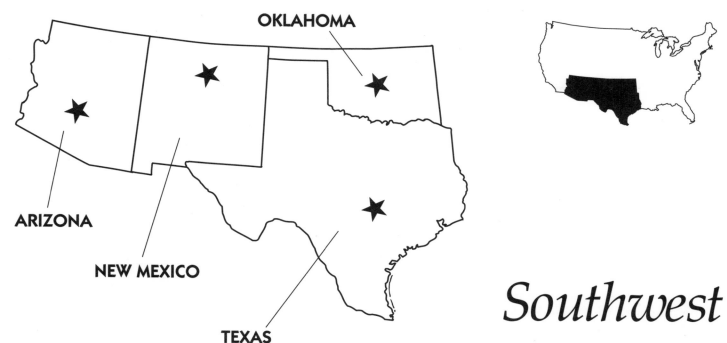

Southwest

There are only four states in this region, but they make up a large chunk of the country. A little of this land came to the U.S. as part of the Louisiana Purchase. More came as a result of the Mexican War, a bit was bought from Mexico in the Gadsden Purchase, and Texas, having won its independence from Mexico on its own in 1836, was admitted as a state in 1845.

Arizona

(AZ)

Capital: Phoenix
State Bird: Cactus Wren
State Flower: Saguaro Cactus Blossom
State Tree: Palo Verde

48th state to enter the Union (February 14, 1912) ★ 6th largest state

It's hard to think about Arizona without thinking about the Grand Canyon. And it's hard to think about the Grand Canyon without thinking about one of the most remarkable men in the history of the American West, John Wesley Powell.

Powell had lost an arm in the Civil War, but this injury hardly slowed him down. After the war, he headed west to lead scientific expeditions on behalf of the government. His most famous journey began at Green River City, Wyoming, and headed south through Glenn Canyon and, eventually, the Grand Canyon. His expedition traveled in four boats—three 21-footers made of oak, and a lightweight 16-footer made of pine, which Powell named after his wife, Emma Dean (who was just about as tough as her husband, and had already become the first white woman to climb Pike's Peak).

At one point, Powell managed to get stranded part way up a steep cliff. He was saved by one of his men, who stripped off his clothes and lowered his long johns as a rescue rope.

By the time they made it to the end of the Grand Canyon, which Powell called "The Great Unknown," they had explored the Green and Colorado Rivers, and much of the land on either side.

Powell later became the head of the National Geologic Survey. As always, he didn't follow maps—he made them!

Phoenix, Arizona

Even though the **phoenix** can rise from the ashes, it had better be careful rising through the **arrow zone** or it might get shot!

The **phoenix** (Phoenix) rises through the **arrow zone** (Arizona).

New Mexico's population is almost  sand dunes—the world's biggest gypsum desert ★

New Mexico
(NM)

Capital: Santa Fe
State Bird: Roadrunner
State Flower: Yucca Flower
State Tree: Pinon

47th state to enter the Union (January 6, 1912) ★ 5th largest state

Almost 1,500 years ago, Native Americans now known as "Anasazis" or "ancient ones" settled in Chaco Canyon in northwest New Mexico. They were farmers, who planted and harvested corn. But they were also builders, who built some of the most amazing and beautiful structures anywhere.

In about 920, they began building what we now call Pueblo Bonito (beautiful village), one of what would eventually be 12 pueblos in the canyon. By 1100, Pueblo Bonito was finished. It was a huge, D-shaped structure with 800 rooms—in fact, it remained the largest apartment house in America until a bigger one was built in New York City in the late 1800s.

The people who built the pueblos at Chaco Canyon were clearly skilled, well-organized, and a dominant force in the region. But soon after Pueblo Bonito was finished, the Anasazi vanished. Some think they were forced away by drought. Some believe they were pushed out by invaders. Others think they created an environmental disaster by cutting down the tens of thousands of trees that they used as roof beams.

The mystery of their disappearance will probably never be solved, but the evidence of their skill remains in the stones of Pueblo Bonito.

Connected to Mexico City by El Camino Real (the royal road), now the oldest road in the U.S.

Santa Fe, New Mexico

Just in time for Christmas and all those thirsty holiday guests, you can get a huge bottle of **new maxi Coke**® which is decorated with **Santa's face**.

Santa's face
(Santa Fe) on a
new maxi Coke®
(New Mexico).

Oklahoma
(OK)

Capital: Oklahoma City
State Bird: Scissor-tailed Flycatcher
State Flower: Mistletoe
State Tree: Redbud

46th state to enter the Union (November 16, 1907) ★ 18th largest state

Much of Oklahoma was once known as "Indian Territory." Native Americans from the east were forced along the "Trail of Tears" to land no one else wanted at the time. After a while, "The Five Civilized Tribes"—Cherokee, Choctaw, Chickasaw, Creek, and Seminole—each had their own chunk of the territory, and their own governments.

Soon, though, white people did want that part of the country, and Indian Territory was opened up to the settlers in a series of Land Rushes. The biggest of these took place at noon on April 22, 1889, when two million acres of land were made available.

Fifty-thousand people crowded onto the territory's borders waiting for the pistol shot that would allow them to race into the territory to stake claims. Overnight, towns sprang up on the plains. Oklahoma City was founded and grew to a population of 10,000—all in a single day!

Some settlers cheated and sneaked onto the land sooner than they should have. They gave Oklahoma its nickname: the Sooner State.

Oklahoma City, Oklahoma

When okras go to visit, they take their homes with them. So, **okra's home is sitting** next to **okra's home**.

Okra's home is sitting (Oklahoma City) next to **okra's home** (Oklahoma).

Texas
(TX)

Capital: Austin
State Bird: Mockingbird
State Flower: Bluebonnet
State Tree: Pecan

28th state to enter the Union (December 29, 1845) ★ 2nd largest state

The Alamo is the most famous battle of the war for Texas independence. But to gain their freedom from Mexico, the Texans actually had to *win* an important fight, and the Battle of San Jacinto was it.

After the Alamo, and the slaughter of the garrison at Goliad, Sam Houston called for more volunteers and began a long retreat, keeping his men clear of the thousands commanded by the Mexican leader, General Santa Ana. Santa Ana gradually split his forces, and Houston finally found his chance to fight on nearly equal terms on the banks of the San Jacinto River near modern-day Galveston.

The Texan force attacked when the Mexicans as-

sumed it was too late for a fight. The battle was short but very bloody. Shouting "Remember the Alamo," the Texans pushed hundreds of Mexican soldiers into a bayou behind their camp. They shot hundreds as they thrashed in the water. When the dust had cleared, there were 630 Mexicans dead—almost half of Santa Ana's army. Only nine Texans were dead or mortally wounded. Santa Ana was eventually captured dressed as a common soldier, and he was eventually forced to sign an armistice that led to Texas' freedom.

Houston was wounded in the foot, but lived to become President of Texas and, later, Senator and Governor.

Austin, Texas

If you get too many old **taxis** together, you're going to have a large **oil stain**.

A big **oil stain** (Austin) from leaking **taxis** (Texas).

For a little practice, answer these.

 What dangerous zone is the phoenix rising through?

What type of beverage is Santa's face on?

What is Okra's home sitting next to?

What leaks to cause the oil stain?

What is rising from the ashes through the arrow zone?

What do you put on the new maxi Coke® to sell it around Christmas time?

What is next to the okra's home and is it standing or sitting?

What will the taxis cause if they leak?

MONTANA

IDAHO

WYOMING

NEVADA

UTAH

COLORADO

Mountain

These are all big states, and they all have high mountains, but the terrain varies from the cool northern Rockies of Montana and Idaho to the frying deserts of Nevada. And there are all sorts of high, dry plains in between.

Colorado

(CO)

Capital: Denver
State Bird: Lark Bunting
State Flower: Rocky Mountain Columbine
State Tree: Blue Spruce

38th state to enter the Union (August 1, 1876) ★ **8th largest state**

Just before World War II, a small group of outdoorsmen persuaded the U.S. Army to establish a force of mountain troops. What eventually became the elite 10th Mountain Division—America's "ski troops"—trained at Fort Hale between Vail and Leadville. Early recruits included most of the country's greatest skiers and mountain climbers. The 10th Mountain Division established a distinguished record against the Germans in the mountains of Italy, but never fought on skis. After the war, many 10th Mountain Division men became leaders in the growing ski industry.

Nowadays, there is a major ski resort at Vail, and a hut system named for our first mountain troops has been developed in the mountains nearby. If you have good skills on skis, and you don't mind carrying your own food and gear, you can follow the 10th Mountain Division Trail, spending the nights at huts all the way from Vail to Aspen, another great downhill skiers' mecca. The huts are heated with woodstoves and have kitchens where you can prepare your food—pretty elegant stuff for the backcountry. Depending on the weather and your fitness, huts can be as close as a couple of hours apart, or as far as 12 hours or more. All this can be great fun—as long as you are fit, well-equipped, and skilled. And now you can do it in the summer, too—on mountain bikes.

Denver, Colorado

Relaxing in his **den** covered with **fur**, the lion listens to his **collar radio**.

A rich lion has a **den** of **fur** (Denver) and a **collar radio** (Colorado).

Idaho
(ID)

Capital: Boise
State Bird: Mountain Bluebird
State Flower: Syringa (Mock Orange)
State Tree: Western White Pine

43rd state to enter the Union (July 3, 1890) ★ 13th largest state

---

In the mid-1930s, a man named Averill Harriman, who later became governor of New York and an important diplomat and statesman, was the chairman of the board of directors of the Union Pacific Railroad.

He asked one of his employees to ride the rails all over the Rocky Mountain west to find the best place to build something new—a big "destination" ski resort. Harriman felt that such a place would encourage people to ride his trains to get to it.

The site that was chosen became Sun Valley, near Ketcham, Idaho. Harriman put his engineers to work, and before long they had designed the slopes, built the lodge buildings, and constructed the world's first chair lift (which they modeled on banana conveyors).

Great skiers from Europe were imported to be instructors, and great chefs came to staff the new hotels. Sun Valley quickly caught on with those rich enough in the depression years to make the trip and pay for their stay. Movie stars were always having their pictures taken on the slopes. To this day, Sun Valley is among the great ski resorts of the world.

(which forms the border between Idaho & Oregon), is the deepest gorge in North America—7,900 feet from its rim to the river

Boise, Idaho

Boy, they're hungry! These **boys** will even **eat a hoe**.

Boys (Boise) will **eat a hoe** (Idaho).

Montana
(MT)

Capital: Helena
State Bird: Western Meadow Lark
State Flower: Bitterroot
State Tree: Ponderosa Pine

41st state to enter the Union (November 8, 1889) ★ 4th largest state

The man we remember as Chief Joseph was called *Hin-mah-too-yah-lat-kekht* by his own people—"thunder traveling to loftier mountain heights." Joseph was a Nez Percé Indian. (Usually pronounced "nez purse" by Americans, this means "pierced nose," because some men of the tribe inserted shells into small slits they made in their noses.)

In 1877, after a series of broken treaties and promises, and a bloody skirmish with the army, the Nez Percé decided to go to Montana, where their friends, the Crows, would help them. On the trip, Joseph's job was to protect the women, the children and the old men who couldn't fight. They were followed by the army, and fought a series of costly battles, each time escaping. When they realized that there would be no peace for them in Montana, the band headed for Canada. They were finally cornered just 40 miles from the border, on Snake Creek near the Bearpaws. Joseph had seen many of his people die, and was worried more would die soon. He felt he had no choice but to surrender. His words have become famous:

"The little children are freezing to death. My people...have no blankets, no food. Hear me, my chiefs! I am tired. My heart is sick and sad. From where the sun now stands I will fight no more forever."

Helena, Montana

Ooh, I bet that hurts! There's a **heel in a man tanning**.

A **heel in a** (Helena) **man tanning** (Montana).

Nevada
(NV)

Capital: Carson City
State Bird: Mountain Bluebird
State Flower: Sagebrush
State Tree: Single-leaf Pinon

36th state to enter the Union (October 31, 1864) ★ 7th largest state

When the Civil War began, many people in Nevada were sympathetic to the Confederacy. One of these was a baker named Reuel Gridley. Gridley lost an election bet and had to pay up by carrying a sack of flour decorated red, white, and blue through the streets of Austin, in the center of Nevada Territory. Somehow, this experience changed Gridley into a supporter of the Union. He auctioned off his flour for $6,000, proceeds to go to the Sanitary Commission, which looked after wounded soldiers, much as the Red Cross would today. The flour was returned to Gridley, and he continued to travel around the region auctioning off his bag of flour over and over.

The part of Nevada around Carson City was incredibly rich in those days, because of the discovery of silver and gold. When Gridley went to this Comstock Load country, the miners of Virginia City and other wealthy mining towns bid over $40,000 for the sack.

Eventually Gridley's bag of flour raised about $275,000. It was the nation's first big charity drive. You can still see the bag of flour at the Nevada Historical Society Museum.

Carson City, Nevada

It's never safe to drink and drive. So, the **car's son is sitting** listening to this dad explain that he can have **no Vodka**.

A **car's son is sitting** (Carson City) and can have **no Vodka** (Nevada).

Utah
(UT)

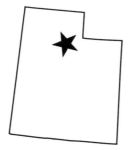

Capital: Salt Lake City
State Bird: Sea Gull
State Flower: Sego Lily
State Tree: Blue Spruce

45th state to enter the Union (January 4, 1896) ★ 11th largest state

In the late 1840s, Brigham Young led a community of Mormons to Utah, where they settled around the Great Salt Lake. They had been forced out of a series of communities in the Midwest. Soon Congress created the Territory of Utah. Young was appointed Governor, but then trouble began between the Mormons and the Federal government. In 1857, President Buchanan sent about 2,500 troops to the Territory, and this triggered what is sometimes called "The Mormon War."

Into the middle of this unpleasantness trundled a wagon train of settlers from Arkansas and Missouri—undoubtedly anti-Mormon—heading for California. A mixed group of Mormon militia and Indians, led by a Mormon called John D. Lee, attacked the wagon train and killed every single adult they found—somewhere between 100 and 120 men, women, and older children died. Only 18 small children were spared.

Brigham Young had not ordered the attack on the wagon trains, but he did try to protect Lee by throwing blame on the Indians alone. The Mormon War ended the next year, with the Mormons retaining real power in the territory while accepting essentially meaningless conditions from Washington.

Salt Lake City, Utah

The **city** around the **salt lake** looks out at the **tall U**.

A **salt lake city** (Salt Lake City) has on its outskirts a **U tall** (Utah).

Wyoming
(WY)

Capital: Cheyenne
State Bird: Meadow Lark
State Flower: Indian Paintbrush
State Tree: Cottonwood

44th state to enter the Union (July 10, 1890) ★ 9th largest state

A man named John Colter walked across the country as part of the Lewis and Clark Expedition, and on the way back, he asked to be allowed to leave the troop to go off with two trappers. He was given permission, and so became the first of what came to be known as "Mountain Men." Colter later found and described the geysers and hot springs of the Yellowstone country of what is now northwestern Wyoming.

As time went on, more and more men headed to the western mountains and lived a rugged life—men like Broken Hand Fitzpatrick, Jim Bridger, Kit Carson, Jedediah, Smith and many others. They were trappers, not explorers, but their travels took them all over the American West, and they often became guides for later waves of pioneers.

Periodically, these mountain men would meet at a *Rendezvous*—a gathering. One of the most famous and most beautiful Rendezvous locations is Jackson Hole, in the Teton country just south of Yellowstone. Here and at other spots, trappers would trade pelts for supplies. They would also gamble, drink, fight, and compete at shooting, running, and riding. It was a big, rough party for the raw, tough men who opened up the country for settlement by the ranchers who followed.

The Johnson County Cattle War in 1892 was a serious shoot-'em-up between big cattlemen and settlers ★ to grant women the right to vote

Devil's Tower (which you saw in the movie "E.T.") is in northeastern Wyoming ★ World

The first state ★ The National Elk Refuge is in Jackson Hole ★ The National Elk Refuge is in Jackson Hole ★ famous geyser "Old Faithful" is at Yellowstone National Park ★

100

Cheyenne, Wyoming

A **shy ant** normally will live in a home built in the shape of a Y—a **Y home**.

A **shy ant** (Cheyenne) in a **Y home** (Wyoming).

Let's see how you do.

What does the lion listen to in his den of fur?

What will the boys do when they are really, really hungry?

If you didn't like people with sunburns, you would put a heel in a what?

What does the car tell the car's son sitting about drinking?

What large letter is on the outskirts of the salt lake city?

In what type of home does the shy ant live?

What's on the walls of the lion listening to his collar radio?

Who will eat a hoe when they are really hungry?

What is in the back of the man tanning?

Who gets told by his dad, "No Vodka!"?

What is the U tall next to?

What little animal lives in the Y home?

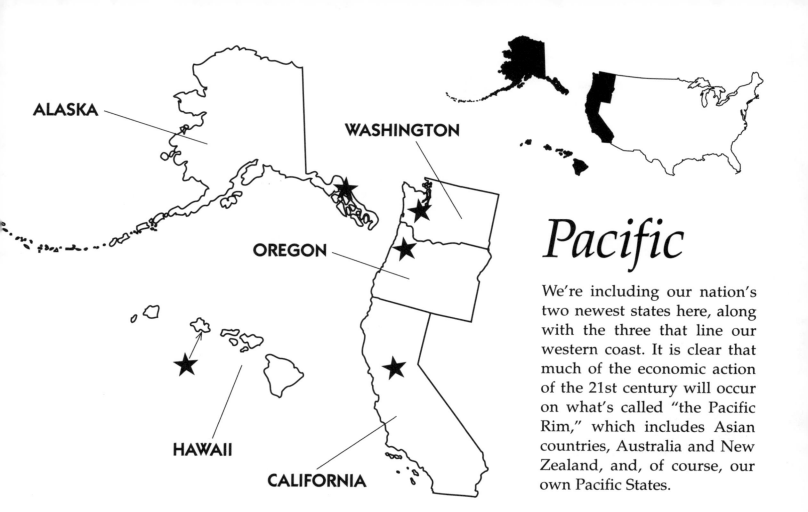

ALASKA

WASHINGTON

OREGON

HAWAII

CALIFORNIA

Pacific

We're including our nation's two newest states here, along with the three that line our western coast. It is clear that much of the economic action of the 21st century will occur on what's called "the Pacific Rim," which includes Asian countries, Australia and New Zealand, and, of course, our own Pacific States.

Alaska
(AK)

Capital: Juneau
State Bird: Willow Ptarmigan
State Flower: Forget-me-not
State Tree: Sitka Spruce

49th state to enter the Union (January 3, 1959) ★ **1st largest state**

The highest mountain in North America is officially named Mount McKinley after William McKinley, our 25th President. But most Alaskans and many others prefer to call it by its original Indian name, Denali, which means "The Great One" or "The High One.". The mountain, which is part of Denali National Park, has two distinct peaks. The North Peak is 19,470 feet high. The South Peak is a little higher, at 20,320 feet.

Many people climb Denali every year. Most of them are flown by skilled bush pilots in small planes onto the Kahiltna Glacier from the little town of Talkeetna. There they set up base camp, wait for good weather, and then trudge up the mountain, often ferrying gear from camp to camp. Other climbers attempt different and even more difficult routes.

Because of its harsh winds and weather, Denali is one of the most dangerous frequently-climbed mountains in the world. Many climbers have died on the mountain, and many others have been saved by heroic rescuers.

Dr. Frederick A. Cook claimed to have climbed Denali in 1906, but those claims were soon questioned, and are seriously doubted today based on a study of photographs. A party of Fairbanks miners reached the North Peak in 1910, and the higher South Peak was reached in 1913.

★ Seward bought Alaska from the Russians in 1867 for $7.2 million, or two cents an acre ★ Alaska was called "Seward's Folly"

104

Juneau, Alaska

He is so in love with the girl with the **jewel nose**, that he thinks, "**I'll ask her** to marry me."

If she has a **jewel nose** (Juneau), **I'll ask her** (Alaska).

California

(CA)

Capital: Sacramento
State Bird: California Valley Quail
State Flower: Golden Poppy
State Tree: California Redwood

31st state to enter the Union (September 9, 1850) ★ 3rd largest state

In the late 1860s, a prospector named William S. Bodie discovered a rich vein of gold near Mono Lake close to the Nevada border. He didn't last long—he went out in a blizzard and was never seen again—but the town he established became one of the roughest, toughest, wildest mining towns of the West.

Because it was far from the law, close to the state line, and full of gold dust, Bodie attracted all sorts of violent, unscrupulous characters who were interested in making a quick buck. Robberies and murders were common. Bodie was called "a shooters town" by the Sacramento Union newspaper, and one observer said that it witnessed an average of six fatal shootings a week during the 1880s. Mark Twain covered the area for a while as a journalist, and he said that "the smoke of battle almost never clears away completely in Bodie."

Bodie's mines played out as the century came to an end, and a big fire in 1897 destroyed much of its main street. But you can still go to Bodie. It's a National Historic Site, protected and maintained by the federal government as a ghost town.

Sacramento, California

After touring all of the National Parks and Monuments and filling her **sack** with **mementos**, the **cow will phone you**.

With a **sack of mementos** (Sacramento), the **cow will phone you** (California).

Hawaii
(HI)

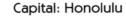

Capital: Honolulu
State Bird: Nene (Hawaiian Goose)
State Flower: Hibiscus
State Tree: Kukui (Candlenut)

50th state to enter the Union (August 21, 1959) ★ 47th largest state

W hen Captain Cook "discovered" the islands, he saw the Hawaiians doing something people come from all over the world to do there now—surfing. One of his officers wrote about it in 1779:

Whenever, from stormy weather, or any extraordinary swell at sea, the impetuosity of the surf is increased to its utmost height, they choose that time for this amusement, which is performed in the following manner:—Twenty or thirty of the natives, taking each a long narrow board, rounded at the ends, set out together from the shore. The first wave they meet they plunge under, and suffering it to roll over them, rise again beyond it…. As soon as they have gained, by these repeated efforts, the smooth water beyond the surf, they lay themselves at length on their board, and prepare for their return…. [T]heir first object is to place themselves on the summit of the largest surge, by which they are driven along with amazing rapidity toward the shore…. The coast being guarded by a chain of rocks, with here and there a small opening between them, they are obliged to steer their board through one of these, or, in case of failure, to quit it before they reach the rocks…. This is reckoned very disgraceful….

Honolulu,
Hawaii

Some roads are straight, some are crooked. But **Highway E** is where the **honey** trucks make **loop loops**.

Honey loop loops (Honolulu) are on **Highway E** (Hawaii).

Oregon
(OR)

Capital: Salem
State Bird: Western Meadow Lark
State Flower: Oregon Grape
State Tree: Douglas Fir

33rd state to enter the Union (February 14, 1859) ★ **10th largest state**

You know how common it is to see people in T-shirts and shorts or tights running or jogging along the streets or through the parks? Some of these folks are serious racers, but most of them are just trying to stay fit and healthy. Did you know that just a generation ago, you almost never saw anyone exercising that way, and you definitely never saw anyone togged out in "official" running clothes or fancy, expensive shoes—this stuff just didn't exist.

Eugene, Oregon, is one of the birthplaces of the American running and fitness boom that started in the early 1970s. Bill Bowerman, the great track coach at the University of Oregon, really got the ball rolling when he came back from a trip to New Zealand, where he had seen and participated in the citizen fun runs another coaching great, Arthur Lydiard, had established there. You can go to Eugene today and find miles of well-maintained, well-used public running trails. Bowerman also co-founded the Nike shoe company. The story goes that he used the family waffle iron to invent a revolutionary new sole for racing and training shoes. Hope he cleaned it up afterwards.

Salem, Oregon

The **sailor's oar is gone**, causing him to row in a circle.

The **sailor's** (Salem) **oar is gone** (Oregon).

Washington
(WA)

Capital: Olympia
State Bird: Willow Goldfinch
State Flower: Coast Rhododendron
State Tree: Western Hemlock

42nd state to enter the Union (November 11, 1889) ★ **20th largest state**

Mount St. Helens was a spectacular, perfect, cone-shaped volcanic peak in Washington's Cascade Mountains. In late 1979, it started rumbling and venting puffs of steam and ash. Scientists knew that an eruption would probably come soon, but they had no idea it would be as spectacular and violent as it was.

On May 18, 1980, Mount St. Helens exploded. The eruption caused a landslide, which in turn let ash and gas burst *sideways* rather that straight up in the air. The ash immediately turned the whole area pitch black, and with the released gas, suffocated 63 people. Forests as far as 20 miles away were flattened or stripped, and all sorts of animals, from insects to large game, were killed. Crops were ruined. The glacier at the top of the mountain melted almost immediately, and ran off into nearby rivers. Floods and mud slides carried away cars, bridges, and houses. Yakima, the nearest city, was covered in a layer of ash.

When the ash cleared, people could see that Mount St. Helens was a perfect cone no more. The top 1,300 feet of the mountain was simply gone. In its place was a crater over a mile across. This was the first volcanic eruption in the lower 48 states since Lassen Peak erupted in 1921, but scientists expect that Mount St. Helens will erupt again in the future.

Corporation, which makes big airliners like the 747, is located in Seattle ★ On a clear day, you can see Mt. Ranier from downtown

Olympia, Washington

One of the new events in the **Olympics** is to see how fast you can **wash a ton**.

At the **Olympics** (Olympia), **wash a ton** (Washington).

Let's see what you remember.

What does the young man think when he sees the jewel-nosed girl?

After collecting a sack of mementos, who will do what?

 Where can the honey trucks do loop loops?

Why is the sailor unhappy?

What is the new event at the Olympics?

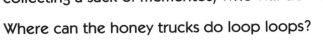

 What does the girl have that makes a man think, "I'll ask her to marry me!"?

What must she have before the cow will phone you?

What do the trucks do on Highway E?

 Whose oar is gone?

Where do they compete in the wash a ton event?

★ *Just For Fun* ★

Here's a Jeopardy-style quiz to test your general knowledge about states and capitals. Some of the information can be found earlier in this book, and some can't. The answers—er, questions—are at the end. Have fun!

1. The world's tallest building stands in this state.

2. The Comstock Load was discovered in this state.

3. This state was once the "Grizzly Bear Republic."

4. This state capital was named after Queen Anne.

5. This state is often called the "Nutmeg State."

6. This is the state in which the Declaration of Independence was signed.

7. This state has the shortest seacoast of any state that has a seacoast.

8. This state was once known as "Indian Territory."

9. This city is the oldest seat of government in the U.S.

10. This is the largest city in the country.

11. This state worries about the San Andreas Fault.

12. This state touches four of the five Great Lakes.

13. This is the "First State."

14. This is the "Sunshine State."

15. This is where Aaron Burr killed Alexander Hamilton in a duel.

16. This state is named after our seventh President.

17. This city was destroyed by Sherman's army.

18. This state is an archipelago.

19. This state has the Mississippi River as its eastern boundary and the Missouri as most of its western boundary.

20. This state's official bird is the Roadrunner. Beep-beep!

21. This state contains the "wild west" towns of Dodge City and Abilene.

22. This city holds America's most famous auto race.

23. This is where you'll find Fort Knox, where much of the country's gold reserves reside.

24. This state has the highest population density in the U.S.

25. This is the smallest state west of the Mississippi.

26. This state is the home of Tabasco Sauce and Huey Long.

27. This city is the location of the United States Naval Academy.

28. This state capital is named after our 16th President.

29. This is the state in which you can find the Petrified Forest.

30. The population center of the United States is in this state.

31. This is the "Mountaineer State."

32. The official bird of this state is the sea gull.

33. This capital was first known as Fort Orange.

34. This is the "Sooner State."

35. A battleship named for this state blew up in Havana Harbor, precipitating the Spanish-American War.

36. This capital was named after a French trapper.

37. This state was the home of Ethan Allen and his Green Mountain Boys.

38. This state was the site of the first English colony in what became the United States.

39. This state was the site of the first successful English colony in what became the United States.

40. This state is the home of Glacier National Park.

41. This was the first state to let women vote.

42. This state contains the geographic center of North America.

43. You could find the Cowboy Hall of Fame in this state capital.

44. This state is the home of Father Flanagan's Boys Town.

45. This is the state in which the Exxon Valdez oil spill occurred.

46. This is where you would find ski areas like Vail and Aspen.

47. The strongest winds ever recorded on Earth blew here.

48. This is the state where you could find "Silicon Valley."

49. This city was home to the "Charter Oak."

50. This is the "Hawkeye State."

51. This is where you could canoe down the Allagash.

52. This state was at the end of the northern pioneer trail.

53. These capitals were also capitals of the Confederacy.

54. Little League Baseball was founded in this state.

55. This state has a "unicam."

56. This is the "Badger State."

57. This capital city is named after the lake it is near.

58. The state capital is named after our third President.

59. This is the country's smallest state.

60. This is the state where you'll find the headwaters of the Missouri River.

61. This state has the longest official name of any state.

62. The first shots of the Civil War were fired in this state.

63. The Wright brothers were born in this state.

64. This state contains the geographical center of the U.S.

65. This is the "Volunteer State."

66. This state is home of the source of the Mississippi.

67. This state has a "panhandle" squeezed between Washington and Montana.

68. This state is the home of the Johnson Space Center.

69. This state is known as the "Mother of Presidents."

70. This is the only state named after a President.

71. This city calls itself "The Hub."

72. This is the only state to have seceded from a seceding state.

73. This is the only state capital in which you can find a royal palace.

74. This state was the site of the northern-most land action of the Civil War.

75. The highest Mountain east of the Mississippi is in this state.

? ? ? ? ?

1. What is Illinois?
2. What is Nevada?
3. What is California?
4. What is Annapolis, Maryland?
5. What is Connecticut?
6. What is Pennsylvania?
7. What is New Hampshire?
8. What is Oklahoma?
9. What is Santa Fe, New Mexico?
10. What is Juneau, Alaska?
11. What is California?
12. What is Michigan?
13. What is Delaware?
14. What is Florida?
15. What is New Jersey?
16. What is Jackson, Mississippi?
17. What is Atlanta, Georgia?
18. What is Hawaii?
19. What is Iowa?
20. What is New Mexico?
21. What is Kansas?
22. What is Indianapolis, Indiana?
23. What is Kentucky?
24. What is New Jersey?
25. What is Arkansas?
26. What is Louisiana?
27. What is Annapolis, Maryland?
28. What is Lincoln, Nebraska?
29. What is Arizona?
30. What is Missouri?
31. What is West Virginia?
32. What is Utah?
33. What is Albany, New York?
34. What is Oklahoma?
35. What is Maine?
36. What is Pierre, South Dakota?
37. What is Vermont?
38. What is North Carolina?
39. What is Virginia?
40. What is Montana?
41. What is Wyoming?
42. What is North Dakota?
43. What is Oklahoma City, Oklahoma?
44. What is Nebraska?
45. What is Alaska?
46. What is Colorado?
47. What is New Hampshire?
48. What is California?
49. What is Hartford, Connecticut?
50. What is Iowa?
51. What is Maine?
52. What is Oregon?
53. What are Montgomery, Alabama, and Richmond, Virginia?
54. What is Pennsylvania?
55. What is Nebraska?
56. What is Wisconsin?
57. What is Salt Lake City, Utah?
58. What is Jefferson City, Missouri?
59. What is Rhode Island?
60. What is Montana?
61. What is Rhode Island?
62. What is South Carolina?
63. What is Ohio?
64. What is South Dakota?
65. What is Tennessee?
66. What is Minnesota?
67. What is Idaho?
68. What is Texas?
69. What is Virginia?
70. What is Washington?
71. What is Boston, Massachusetts?
72. What is West Virginia?
73. What is Honolulu, Hawaii?
74. What is Vermont?
75. What is North Carolina?

★ Name That State ★

Alabama   Hawaii   Massachusetts   New Mexico   South Dakota
Alaska   Idaho   Michigan   New York   Tennessee
Arizona   Illinois   Minnesota   North Carolina   Texas
Arkansas   Indiana   Mississippi   North Dakota   Utah
California   Iowa   Missouri   Ohio   Vermont
Colorado   Kansas   Montana   Oklahoma   Virginia
Connecticut   Kentucky   Nebraska   Oregon   Washington
Delaware   Louisiana   Nevada   Pennsylvania   West Virginia
Florida   Maine   New Hampshire   Rhode Island   Wisconsin
Georgia   Maryland   New Jersey   South Carolina   Wyoming

119

Bibliography

Aten, Jerry. *Fifty Nifty States.* Columbus, OH: Good Apple, 1990.

Aten, Jerry. *America: From Sea to Shining Sea.* Columbus, OH: Good Apple, 1988.

Aylesworth, Thomas. *Kid's World Almanac of the 50 States.* Mahwah, NJ: World Almanac, 1990.

Bacon, Josephine. *Doubleday Atlas of the United States of America.* New York: Doubleday, 1990.

Black, S. *Fabulous Facts About Fifty States.* New York: Scholastic Inc., 1991.

Brandt, Sue. *Facts About the 50 States.* Danbury, CT: Watts, 1988.

Brandt, Sue. *State Trees: Including the Commonwealth of Puerto Rico.* Danbury, CT: Watts, 1992.

Caney, Steven. *Steven Caney's Kid's America.* New York: Workman, 1978.

Carpenter, Allan. *Enchantment of America series.* 50 volumes. Danbury, CT: Children's Press, 1978.

Dowden, Anne. *State Flowers.* New York: HarperCollins, 1978.

Garrison, Edward. *Short Stories About States and Capitals.* Hamlet, NC: EG Photoprint, date not set.

Krulik, Nancy. *All About the Fifty States: A Picture Puzzle Book.* New York: Scholastic Inc., 1992.

Lancaster, Derek. *Picture America: States and Capitals.* Salt Lake City: Compact Classics, 1991.

Landau, Elaine. *State Birds: Including the Commonwealth of Puerto Rico.* Danbury, CT: Watts, 1992.

Landau, Elaine. *State Flowers: Including the Commonwealth of Puerto Rico.* Danbury, CT: Watts, 1992.

Santrey, Laurence. *State and Local Government.* Mahwah, NJ: Troll Associates, 1985.

Silvani, Harold. *States and Capitals.* Cypress, CA: Creative Teaching, 1975.